The Really Wild Life of Snakes™

CORAL SNAKES

HEATHER FELDMAN

The Rosen Publishing Group's
PowerKids Press™
New York

For Mom and Dad, with love and thanks

Published in 2004 by The Rosen Publishing Group, Inc.
29 East 21st Street, New York, NY 10010

First Edition

Editor: Kathy Kuhtz Campbell
Book Design: Michael de Guzman, Mike Donnellan

Photo Credits: Cover, back cover, pp. 4, 7, 19, 19 (inset) © Charles W. Melton; pp. 4 (inset), 11, 15, 19 © Michael & Patricia Fogden/CORBIS; p. 8 © Bettmann/CORBIS; p. 12 Animals Animals © Breck P. Kent; p. 16 © Jeffrey L. Rotman/CORBIS.

Feldman, Heather.
Coral snakes / Heather Feldman.— 1st ed.
    v. cm. — (The really wild life of snakes)
Contents: Colorful snakes — What are snakes?—Eastern coral snakes—Western coral snakes—Dangerous teeth—Beware of the coral snake—A colorful new skin—Slithering snakes—Coral snake babies—Coral snakes and ants.
  ISBN 0-8239-6719-0 (lib. bdg.)
1. Coral snakes—Juvenile literature. [1. Coral snakes. 2. Snakes.] I. Title. II. Series.
  QL666.O64 F45 2004
  597.96—dc21
                                                2002011373

Manufactured in the United States of America

CONTENTS

COLORFUL SNAKES

Coral snakes are small, brightly colored snakes with black noses. They are members of a family of poisonous snakes that includes cobras and that is called **Elapidae**. There are two main features that set coral snakes apart from other snakes in North America. One is that they inject nerve-attacking **venom** through their short **fangs**. The other is their markings of black, red, and yellow or white rings. These colors serve as a warning sign that coral snakes can cause harm. Some harmless snakes, such as milk snakes, copy the coral snakes' colors. These look-alikes try to make enemies believe that they are as harmful as coral snakes.

Top: *A Mexican milk snake looks similar to a coral snake.*
Bottom: *Coral snakes, such as this western coral snake, have a black nose and red rings that touch yellow or white rings.*

WHAT ARE CORAL SNAKES?

Coral snakes are **reptiles**, as are all snakes. What makes snakes different from other reptiles? Snakes do not have arms and legs. Their muscles and scales help them to move along the ground. Snakes do not have eyelids. They have a clear scale that covers each eye. Snakes cannot hear the way other reptiles do. They have no outer ears. Instead they feel **vibrations** in the ground or in the water by using the bones in their skulls. These bones send the vibrations to the inner ears. The vibrations let the snakes know whether an animal is moving toward them or away from them. This sense helps snakes when they are hunting their **prey**.

The clear scale that covers each eye on a coral snake is called a spectacle. Unlike most poisonous snakes, which have catlike pupils, a coral snake has round pupils in its small, black eyes.

SNAKEBITE
THE WORD "CORAL" REFERS TO A KIND OF RED STONE ONCE FOUND IN THE MEDITERRANEAN SEA.

RANGE OF WESTERN CORAL SNAKES

RANGE OF EASTERN CORAL SNAKES

WHERE DO CORAL SNAKES LIVE?

There are more than 50 **species** of coral snakes living in areas around the world, including in Africa, Asia, and South America. Only two species live in North America. These are the eastern coral snake and the western coral snake. Eastern coral snakes live in the southeastern United States. They live in pine and oak forests and near swamps and riverbanks. The western coral snake is a rare species that lives in the southwestern United States and in parts of Mexico. Western coral snakes make their homes in rocky areas, on mountain slopes, and in desert areas, where they use the **saguaro** cactus for shelter.

Eastern coral snakes are also called harlequin snakes because of their bright colors. A harlequin is a type of clown who wears a brightly colored costume.

9

SMALL SNAKES WITH RINGS OF COLOR

An adult eastern coral snake is about 2 ½ feet (76 cm) in length. It has a black head and a yellow and black tail. Red, yellow, and black rings of color wrap around the rest of its body. A full-grown western coral snake is usually 1 ½ feet (46 cm) long. It has yellow or white rings that are wider than an eastern coral snake's. Most coral snakes are **nocturnal**, or active at night. They eat small snakes, lizards, and frogs. They have smaller mouths than do most other snakes. They cannot open their mouths wide to eat large prey. Still they can cause great harm, even to large animals, because their venom is very powerful.

This western coral snake is eating a crowned snake. Western coral snakes are also called Arizona or Sonoran coral snakes because they live in the Sonoran Desert of Arizona.

SNAKEBITE
USE THE RHYME "RED TOUCH YELLOW, KILL A FELLOW" TO REMEMBER THAT A CORAL SNAKE HAS POISON.

BEWARE OF THE BITE!

A coral snake has a fang on each side of its upper jaw. Its fangs are longer than its other teeth. A coral snake's fangs are short compared to those of other poisonous snakes. A coral snake's fangs are fixed in place rather than being folded against the roof of its mouth, as are the fangs of a rattlesnake. When a coral snake bites, its fangs push venom into its victim. A coral snake's venom **glands** make mostly **neurotoxins**. These **substances** attack a prey's **nervous system**. As it spreads through the bloodstream, the venom **paralyzes** muscles until the prey's heart and lungs stop working. Then the coral snake can eat its prey.

Coral snakes use a little venom when they bite small prey, such as small snakes, and more venom when they bite larger prey, such as mice. They can take about an hour to swallow prey.

HIDDEN SNAKES

Coral snakes do not attack if they are left alone. Poisonous snakes usually attack only when they believe that they are in danger. Coral snakes often hide in the sand, under logs, or in plants. They are rarely seen by people. When they are surprised or feel unsafe, coral snakes might hide their heads under their bodies. Sometimes they flatten their bodies to look larger. They might raise their tails to confuse their attackers about which end is their head. They might make a popping sound near the end of their tails to frighten **predators**. They will also bite to protect themselves. If you see a coral snake, you should back away.

This coral snake in Central America is raising its tail to fool an enemy about which end is its head and which is its tail. Many coral snakes perform this trick for their own protection.

SNAKEBITE
MOST BITES FROM
CORAL SNAKES RESULT
FROM PEOPLES'
CARELESS HANDLING
OF CAPTURED SNAKES.
YOU SHOULD NEVER
TRY TO PICK UP A
CORAL SNAKE.

SNAKEBITE
SINCE THE 1950s, ANTIVENIN HAS BEEN USED IN THE UNITED STATES TO TREAT CORAL SNAKE BITES.

HOW TO TREAT A CORAL SNAKE BITE

If a person is bitten by a coral snake, that person should go to a hospital immediately for treatment. A coral snake's venom can affect the working of a person's heart, lungs, and kidneys enough to kill that person. Snakebites are treated with a medicine called antivenin. To make coral snake antivenin, scientists collect venom from a coral snake's fangs. A small amount of the venom is injected into a horse. The horse's body makes **chemicals** to act against the venom. Scientists take some of the horse's blood and separate the chemicals from it. The chemicals are made into the antivenin. A doctor injects the antivenin into a patient to **counteract** the coral snake's venom.

The venom of a krait, a relative of the coral snake, is being collected. The process of taking venom from a snake's fangs is called milking a snake. The venom is used in making antivenin.

A COLORFUL NEW SKIN

One of the most interesting things about snakes is the way they shed their skin. This process is called **molting**. Coral snakes molt when a new layer of skin has grown underneath the outer layer. Adult coral snakes molt between 2 and 10 times every year. Young snakes molt more often because they grow more rapidly. When a coral snake molts, its outer layer of skin turns a dull color. The snake rubs its jaws against rocks to help it push off the loose outer layer of skin. The coral snake slides out of its old skin. This outer layer peels back from the snake's head to its tail. Its new skin is colorful and bright.

Top: *A western coral snake is molting.* Bottom: *It might take it a few minutes or several hours to molt. The old skin is very thin. You can still see the pattern of the snake's scales on the skin.*

SNAKEBITE
THE GROUP OF EGGS THAT A FEMALE CORAL SNAKE LAYS AT ONE TIME IS CALLED A CLUTCH.

CORAL SNAKE BABIES

Most coral snakes **mate** in the spring, but certain kinds of coral snakes mate at other times of the year. After a female and a male mate, the female lays eggs. Eggs are usually laid between May and July. Coral snakes are the only poisonous snakes in North America that lay eggs. Other poisonous snakes, such as rattlesnakes, give birth to live young. A coral snake's eggs are soft yet firm to protect the growing babies. Female western coral snakes lay about 3 eggs. Female eastern coral snakes lay from 3 to 12 eggs. After about two months, the babies hatch. The snakes take care of themselves as soon as they hatch.

Most coral snake eggs are either white or yellow in color and are oval in shape. Babies, such as these in Costa Rica, have a special tooth, called an egg tooth, to help them cut out of the eggs.

CORAL SNAKES AND PEOPLE

Coral snakes are not a danger to people as long as we respect them and do not get too close to them. In years past, state governments paid hunters to slay coral snakes because they were afraid that the snakes would kill people. Many coral snakes were destroyed because of this fear. Today we know that it is unnecessary to kill coral snakes as long as people are educated and treat the snakes with respect. In fact, today doctors are studying coral snake venom to find ways it can be used in treating major illnesses. The coral snake is a beautiful snake, but for most people it is a creature best treasured from a distance!

GLOSSARY

chemicals (KEH-mih-kulz) Matter that can be mixed with other matter to cause changes.

counteract (KOWN-teh-rakt) To act against the effects of something.

Elapidae (EH-leh-pee-dee) The scientific name for the family of poisonous snakes with grooved fangs that includes cobras, kraits, and coral snakes.

fangs (FANGZ) Sharp, hollow, or grooved teeth that inject venom.

glands (GLANZ) Organs of the body that produce a substance to help with a bodily function.

mate (MAYT) To join together to make babies.

molting (MOHLT-ing) Shedding hair, feathers, shell, horns, or skin.

nervous system (NER-vus SIS-tum) A system of nerve fibers in people or animals.

neurotoxins (nur-oh-TOK-senz) Poisonous substances that attack the nerves and nerve tissues.

nocturnal (nok-TER-nul) Active at night.

paralyzes (PAR-uh-lyz-ez) Makes a person or an animal lose feeling or movement in the limbs.

predators (PREH-duh-terz) Animals that kill other animals for food.

prey (PRAY) An animal that is hunted by another animal for food.

reptiles (REP-tylz) Cold-blooded animals with lungs and scales.

saguaro (sah-WER-oh) A type of large cactus. Saguaros are located in the deserts of the southwestern United States and Mexico.

species (SPEE-sheez) A single kind of plant or animal. All people are one species.

substances (SUB-stan-siz) The materials that things are made of.

venom (VEH-num) A poison passed by one animal into another through a bite or a sting.

vibrations (vy-BRAY-shunz) Fast movements up and down or back and forth.

INDEX

WEB SITES

Due to the changing nature of Internet links, PowerKids Press has developed an online list of Web sites related to the subject of this book. This site is updated regularly. Please use this link to access the list:
www.powerkidslinks.com/rwls/coral/